DATE			

MUMMIES

By S.L. Hamilton

VISIT US AT
WWW.ABDOPUBLISHING.COM

Published by ABDO Publishing Company, 8000 West 78th Street, Suite 310, Edina, MN 55439. Copyright ©2011 by Abdo Consulting Group, Inc. International copyrights reserved in all countries. No part of this book may be reproduced in any form without written permission from the publisher. A&D Xtreme™ is a trademark and logo of ABDO Publishing Company.

Printed in the United States of America, North Mankato, Minnesota.
052010
092010

Editor: John Hamilton
Graphic Design: Sue Hamilton
Cover Design: John Hamilton
Cover Photo: Miriam Writer
Interior Photos: AP-pgs 14, 15, 22, 23, 24, 25, 30 & 31; Corbis-pg 10; Getty Images-pgs 8 & 9; Mary Evans Picture Library-pgs 16 & 17; National Georgraphic-pgs 10 & 11; Robert Dalrymple-pgs 26 & 27; Photo Researchers-pgs 1, 4, 5, 6, 7, 12, 13, 18, 19, 20 & 21; Thinkstock-pgs 2, 3, 12 & 14; Universal Studios-pgs 28 & 29.

Library of Congress Cataloging-in-Publication Data

Hamilton, Sue L., 1959-
  Mummies / S.L. Hamilton.
    p. cm. -- (Xtreme monsters)
  Includes index.
  ISBN 978-1-61613-469-3
  1. Mummies--Juvenile literature. I. Title.
  GN293.H35 2011
  393'.3--dc22
                                    2010003293

CONTENTS

XTREME

Supernatural forces bring the dead back to life. These corpses walk the earth as powerful mummies.

MUMMIES

MUMMIES IN

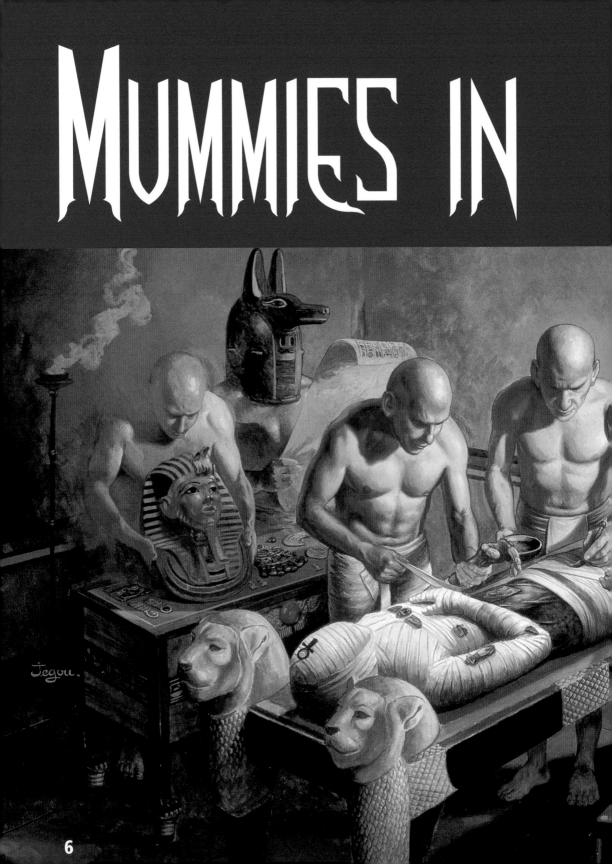

HISTORY

Ancient Egyptians believed in life after death. Their religion taught that the spirit and the body made a dangerous journey to the underworld. Since people needed their bodies in the afterlife, Egyptians used all their skills to preserve the dead.

The best mummification was done for royalty or important, wealthy people.

Tomb Raiders

Wealthy Egyptians were often buried with gold and jewels. Fantastic treasure could be had by anyone brave enough to break into a tomb and steal it. Some graves were hidden and protected by curses. An Egyptian mummy was aboard the HMS *Titanic* when the ship sank in 1912. Some blame the mummy's curse for the ship's sinking.

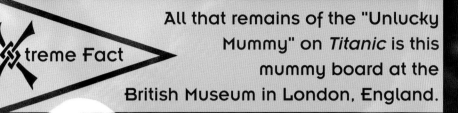

All that remains of the "Unlucky Mummy" on *Titanic* is this mummy board at the British Museum in London, England.

King Tut

Howard Carter

Lord Carnarvon

The most famous Egyptian mummy is King Tutankhamun, also known as King Tut. The teenage king died in 1323 BC. Archeologist Howard Carter found Tut's tomb in November 1922. In April 1923, the man who paid for the dig, Lord Carnarvon, died of an infection. This started untrue rumors of a curse on King Tut's tomb.

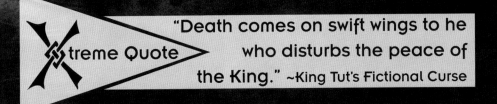

"Death comes on swift wings to he who disturbs the peace of the King." ~King Tut's Fictional Curse

The solid gold coffin of the pharaoh, or king, Tutankhamun.

Becoming

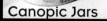

Canopic Jars

A Mummy

To mummify a body, internal organs were removed and put in Canopic jars. The body was dried for 40 days. Once dry, the corpse was stuffed with a preservative called natron, then coated in resin.

"They ripped out your guts and then stuffed them in jars?" ~Rick, *The Mummy*

Wrapping a Mummy

Once the body was embalmed, cosmetics were applied. Next, the body was carefully bandaged. A death mask was placed over the head to provide an image of the person.

King Tut's death mask.

An Egyptian mummy is partially unwrapped and cleaned in a museum.

15

STRENGTHS AND

WEAKNESSES

Fictional mummies sleep until their rest is disturbed. Once they are awake, so are their supernatural powers. Mummies have superior strength and stamina. They never quit. Some can shape-shift into clouds of sand or swarms of beetles. Some command armies of the undead.

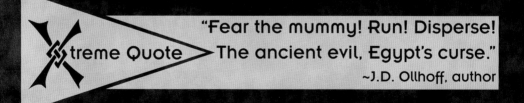

Xtreme Quote

"Fear the mummy! Run! Disperse! The ancient evil, Egypt's curse."
~J.D. Ollhoff, author

Weaknesses

Bullets, knives, and ropes have no effect on mummies. However, the dried-out, resin-coated mummies cannot survive fire. A match or lighter are the best tools for destroying a mummy.

Xtreme Definition

Resin /noun/ A sticky fluid that comes from pine and fir trees. It dries hard in the air and burns very well.

REAL-LIFE

Egypt's ancient royalty are the most famous of mummies. However, preserved bodies from the past have been found in many places around the world.

MUMMIES

South American Mummies

The cold, dry air of South America's Andes Mountains preserved the bodies of some natives. Some recently discovered mummies included three children. They were left high on a volcano as an offering to the gods. The low-oxygen, subfreezing conditions created perfect mummies.

Mummies of three children were found in 1999 at the top of Argentina's Llullaillaco volcano. They were sacrificed to the gods 500 years ago.

Maori Warriors

The Maori tribe of New Zealand were invaded by European explorers in the mid-1700s. Many Maori warriors died. Their tattooed heads were cut off and mummified. These Maori heads were once so popular with European collectors that slaves were tattooed and their heads cut off and sold.

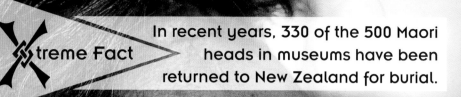

Some salt mummies were so well preserved, they still had food in their stomachs.

Salt Mummies

Salt preserves meat, and humans are no exception. Mummified bodies have been discovered in salt mines in Iran and Austria. The oldest salt mine in the world is in Hallstatt, Austria. In 1734, a mummified miner was found buried in salt from a cave-in 2,500 years ago. "The man in salt" remains in the mine today.

Universal Picture's 1932 film *The Mummy* was the first major mummy movie. It starred Boris Karloff.

In 1944, Lon Chaney Jr. starred in *The Mummy's Ghost.*

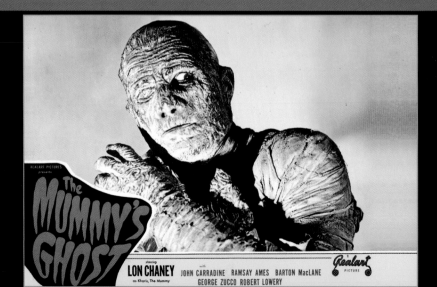

MOVIES

Universal Pictures released a series of popular mummy pictures from 1999 to 2008: *The Mummy, The Mummy Returns,* and *The Mummy: Tomb of the Dragon Emperor.*

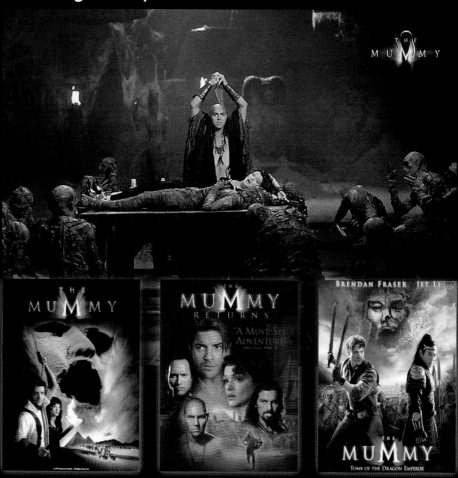

THE

Afterlife
A life believed to happen after a person dies.

Canopic Jars
Jars used by ancient Egyptians to hold the organs of a dead person. The tops sometimes resembled animal heads representing gods.

Corpse
A dead body.

Embalm
A process to keep a dead body from decaying.

Fiction
Stories that are written using an author's imagination.

Mummy Board
The inner lid of an Egyptian coffin.

GLOSSARY

Natron
A naturally occurring powder used to preserve a body during mummification. It is similar to a combination of salt and baking soda.

New Zealand
An island country in the South Pacific.

Preservative
A chemical that keeps a body from decaying.

Tomb
A chamber built for the dead.

Underworld
A dark, dangerous place that Egyptians believed the dead must travel through in order to reach the afterlife.

INDEX